EXPLORING THE UNIVERSE

THE NEAR PLANETS

ROBIN KERROD

RAINTREE
STECK-VAUGHN
PUBLISHERS

A Harcourt Company

Austin   New York
www.raintreesteckvaughn.com

**First American edition published in 2002
by Raintree Steck-Vaughn Publishers**

© 2002 by Graham Beehag Books

Raintree Steck-Vaughn Publishers
4515 Seton Center Parkway
Austin, Texas 78755

Website address: www.raintreesteckvaughn.com

Library of Congress Cataloging-in-Publication Data

Data is available upon request

ISBN 0-7398-2819-3

Printed and bound in the United States.

1 2 3 4 5 6 7 8 9 0 05 04 03 02 01

Contents

Introduction

The Sun rushes headlong through space the solar system in tow. Earth and eight bodies called planets form the major part of the solar system. Each planet circles around the Sun at varying distances from it. In order of distance from the Sun, the nine planets are Mercury, Venus, Earth, Mars, Jupiter, Saturn, Uranus, Neptune, and Pluto.

The four planets nearest the Sun—Mercury, Venus, Earth, and Mars—lie quite close together in space. Often referred to as the inner or near planets, they have much in common. They are very different from the planets farthest from the Sun—Jupiter, Saturn, Uranus, Neptune, and Pluto—which are referred to as the outer or far planets.

The common link between all the near planets is that they are made mainly of rock. That is why they are called terrestrial, or Earth-like, planets. Although they are similar in composition, they are different in size and have developed along different lines since their birth some 4.6 billion years ago.

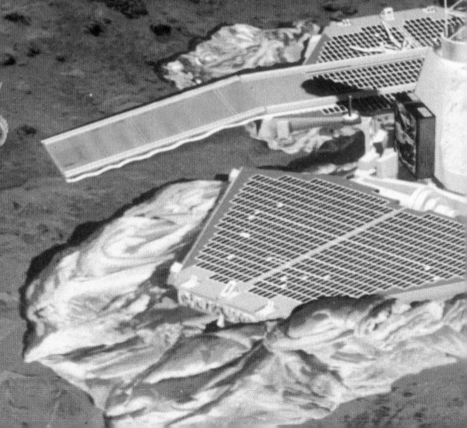

An artist's impression of the *Pathfinder* probe and the *Sojourner* rover on Mars. In the background are the mountains known as the Twin Peaks.

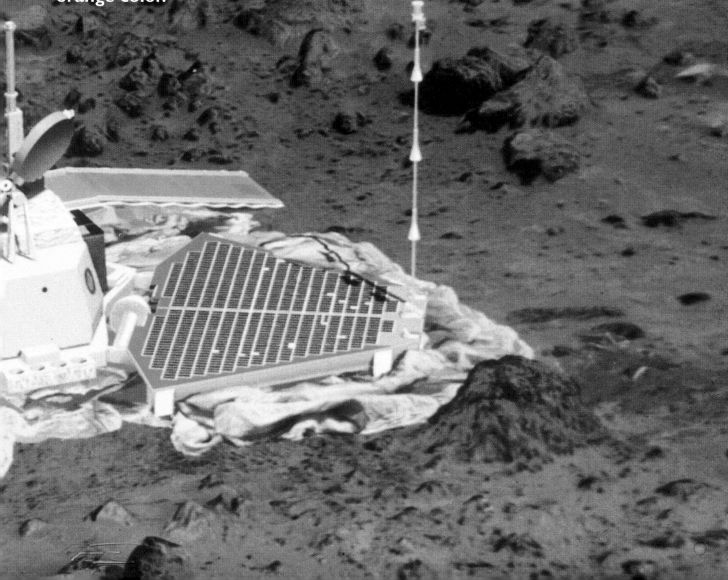

Mercury is the smallest of the inner planets and the one closest to the Sun. It is a scorching world scarred with craters. Temperatures can rise to 840°F (450°C). Venus is the hottest planet with the temperature as high as 900°F (480°C). Its volcanic landscape is hidden from view beneath permanent clouds. Earth is a green and pleasant land thanks to its comfortable temperatures and the presence of liquid water. It is the only planet on which conditions are suitable for life as we know it. Mars is much smaller, and much cooler than Earth.

All the inner planets are visible in the night sky, and their existence has been known since people began gazing at the stars. Venus is the most unmistakable of the planets, hanging like a brilliant star in the west just after sunset on many nights of the year. It is often referred to as the evening star. Mars is distinctive, too, recognizable by its fiery red-orange color.

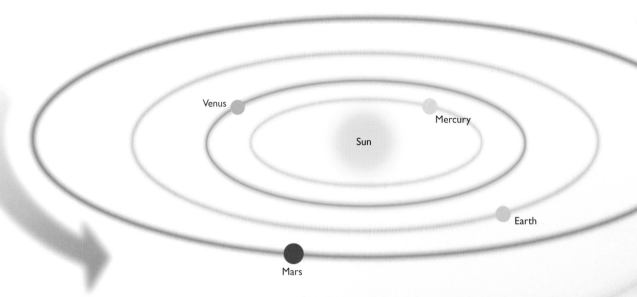

Paths of the Planets

The four inner planets—Mercury, Venus, Earth, and Mars—are located in the center of the solar system. They are relatively close to one another, sometimes passing within a few tens of millions of miles. Venus, for example, sometimes approaches within 26 million miles (42 million kilometers) of Earth.

"Tens of millions of miles" might not seem close, but it is in terms of distances in space. Beyond Mars, space is fairly empty for hundreds of millions of miles until Jupiter. This giant body is the first of the widely scattered outer planets.

The planets circle around the Sun in regular paths, or orbits. The farther away they are from the Sun, the greater the distance they have to travel in their orbit, and the longer is their "year"—the time they take to circle the Sun. Mercury's year lasts only about 88 Earth-days, but Mars's year is nearly eight times longer.

In the Same Direction

As they orbit the Sun, the planets do not move in all directions. They all travel in much the same plane, or flat sheet, in space, and they all circle around the Sun in the same direction—counter clockwise, or in the opposite direction of the way the hands of a clock move.

Above: The four inner planets circle the Sun quite close together. Mars lies on average about 142 million miles (228 million km) away from the Sun, and occasionally comes within 35 million miles (56 million km) of Earth.

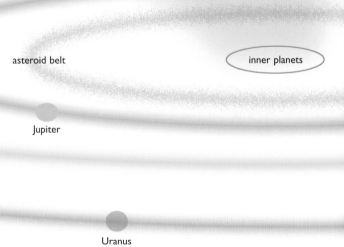

asteroid belt

inner planets

Jupiter

Uranus

Circling in Ovals

Strictly speaking, it is not correct to say that planets "circle" the Sun. The orbits of the planets are an oval, or elliptical, path around the Sun. This means that the planets are closer to the Sun at some points in their orbits than they are at others. Among the inner planets, Mercury and Mars have the most oval, or eccentric, orbits. Mars's distance from the Sun varies between 129 and 155 million miles (207 and 249 million kilometers).

Planet Data

Planet	Av. distance from Sun in million miles (km)	Diameter at Equator in miles (km)	Completes orbit (length of year)	Rotates around in (length of day)	Mass (Earth=1)	Density (water=1)	Number of moons
Mercury	36 (58)	3,032 (4,880)	88 days	58.6 days	0.06	5.4	0
Venus	67 (108)	7,521 (12,104)	225 days	243 days	0.8	5.2	0
Earth	93 (150)	7,927 (12,756)	365.25 days	23.94 hours	1	5.5	1
Mars	142 (228)	4,221 (6,792)	687 days	24.63 hours	0.1	3.9	2
Sun	—	865,000 (1,392,000)	—	25 days	330,000	1.4	—

asteroids

orbit of Pluto

Saturn

The five outer planets are more widely scattered through space. Even the nearest, Jupiter, never comes closer than about 460 million miles (740 million km) to the Sun. And the farthest planet, Pluto, wanders more than 4,500 million miles (7,300 million km) away.

Neptune

Size and Structure

Earth is the largest of the four inner planets. Venus is only slightly smaller. Then comes Mars and finally Mercury, which is only about one-third the size of Earth in diameter. Despite the differences in size between the four planets, astronomers believe that they all have a similar structure, or make-up.

Of course, we only know for certain what Earth is like inside. Geologists—the scientists who study Earth—have found this out by studying the way earthquake waves travel through the rocks. The waves suddenly change direction at different depths underground, indicating that they are passing through different layers.

The geologists have found that Earth is made up of two main layers of rock above a huge ball of molten metal, mainly iron and nickel. This ball forms the core, or center, of Earth. The rock layers above it are the hard crust that forms Earth's surface and a denser layer of rock underneath called the mantle.

The inner planets, drawn to the same scale. The cutaways show how they are made up of different layers.

Looking at Layers

The other inner planets almost certainly have similar layers. But as the cutaway diagrams show, the size of the layers and the core varies widely.

Mercury seems to have only a thin crust and mantle but a huge metal core. Venus probably has a slightly smaller core than Earth but a thicker crust. Earth's core is different from those of the other planets because the outer part is liquid, in the form of molten metal. Scientists believe that this is the reason Earth has such a strong magnetic field in comparison with the other inner planets.

Mars is less dense than all the other inner planets. This indicates that it does not have as much metal in its core.

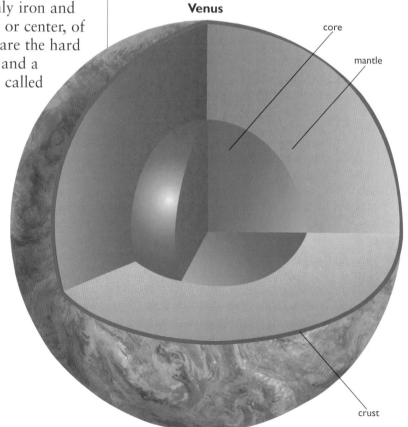

Venus

core

mantle

crust

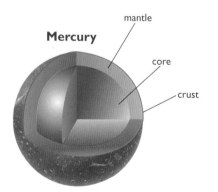

mantle

Mercury

core

crust

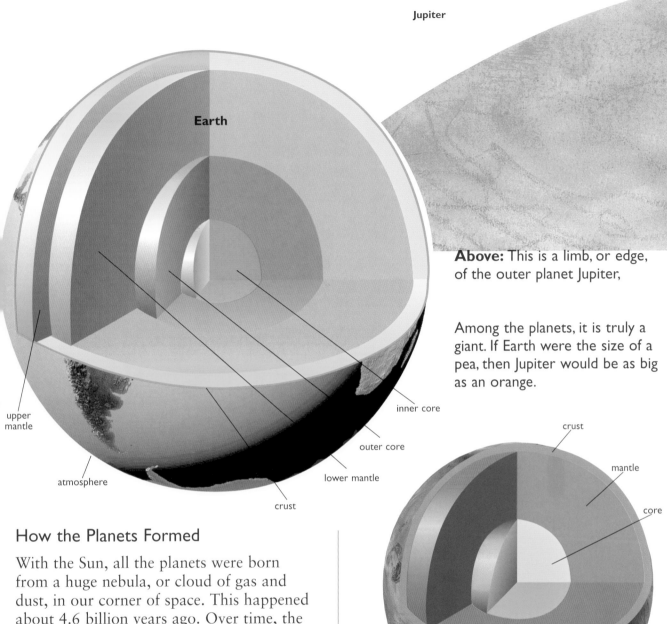

Earth

upper mantle

atmosphere

crust

lower mantle

outer core

inner core

Above: This is a limb, or edge, of the outer planet Jupiter,

Among the planets, it is truly a giant. If Earth were the size of a pea, then Jupiter would be as big as an orange.

crust

mantle

core

Mars

How the Planets Formed

With the Sun, all the planets were born from a huge nebula, or cloud of gas and dust, in our corner of space. This happened about 4.6 billion years ago. Over time, the gas cloud shrunk down into a hot ball (which would become the Sun), surrounded by a disk of matter.

The disk was made up of chunks of rock, metal, gas, and dust. In time the chunks came together to form larger and larger bodies, which gathered around them gas and dust. These were the infant planets.

Blasts of gas and particles from the Sun blew away the gas and dust around the four young inner planets into the outer part of the solar system, leaving them bare rock.

Over time, gases escaped from the rocky surface of the planets through volcanoes to

form new atmospheres. Mercury was too small and too hot to hold on to an atmosphere. Venus and Earth were big enough and had strong enough gravity to keep a thick atmosphere. Being much smaller, Mars could hold on only to a much thinner atmosphere.

SPEEDY MERCURY

Mercury is the closest planet to the Sun. It is also the fastest-moving planet, hurtling along in its orbit at a speed of nearly 30 miles (50 km) a second. Appropriately, it is named after the fleet-footed messenger of the gods in Roman mythology.

Like Venus and Mars, Mercury can be seen from Earth with the naked eye. At best, it looks like a bright star. But it is the most difficult of the inner planets to spot. This is because it never strays far from the Sun in the sky and cannot be seen in really dark conditions.

Mercury can sometimes be seen as a morning star down low near the horizon in the east just before sunrise. In the northern hemisphere, fall is usually the best time to see it in the morning skies. Sometimes Mercury can be seen low in the western sky just after sunset as an evening star. Spring is usually the best time to see it in the evening sky.

Mercury can be seen more easily using binoculars or a telescope. Seen through a telescope, Mercury seems to change size over time. This happens as Mercury approaches Earth and then moves farther away as it makes its orbit around the Sun.

To observers on Earth, Mercury also seems to change shape over time. This is because we see different amounts of it lit up by the Sun at different times as it makes its orbit. We call these changing shapes its phases. They are like the changing shapes, or phases, of the Moon that we see every month.

Telescopes, however, are not powerful enough to show any details of Mercury's surface, except a few vague markings. Astronomers had no idea of what the surface was like until the space probe *Mariner 10* flew past it in 1974. The planet turned out to be almost completely covered in craters, like the ancient highland areas of our Moon.

Left: Craters large and small dominate the surface of Mercury. The largest have central mountain peaks, just like the large lunar craters.

A montage of images sent back by the probe *Mariner 10*. It flew past Mercury three times—twice in 1974 and once in 1975.

The Long Day

Earth takes 24 hours to spin around once on its axis. This period of time is a day. But Mercury spins around much more slowly, taking nearly 59 Earth-days to spin around just once. It takes only 88 Earth-days to travel once around the Sun—this is Mercury's year.

This slow rotation and short "year" give Mercury a very long daytime (when it is in the sunlight) and a very long nighttime (when it is in darkness).

On Earth, there is only one day between one midday and the next. But on Mercury there are 176 Earth-days—in other words a Mercury "day" is 176 Earth-days long. Both daytime and nighttime last for about half this time—88 Earth-days.

Scorching Hot

We would expect Mercury to be a hot planet because it orbits so close to the Sun.

MERCURY DATA

Diameter: 3,032 miles (4,880 km)

Average distance from Sun: 36,000,000 miles (58,000,000 km)

Mass (Earth=1): 0.06

Density (water=1): 5.4

Spins on axis in: 58.6 days

Circles round Sun in: 88 days

Number of moons: 0

During Mercury's long daytime, places are baked by the Sun for 88 Earth-days at a time. Temperatures there soar as high as 430°C, or more than four times the temperature of boiling water. This is hot enough to melt lead.

Make-up of Mercury's incredibly faint atmosphere.

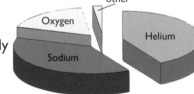

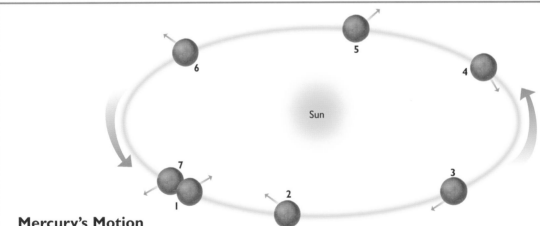

Mercury's Motion

The diagram shows how Mercury slowly spins around, as it orbits, or rotates around, the Sun. In position 1, the arrow on Mercury points directly toward the Sun. We can call this midday on Mercury. As the planet travels in its orbit, the arrow points in different directions. In 1 Mercury "year" of 88 days (7), it has spun round 1½ times, and the arrow is now pointing directly away from the Sun into the darkness. We can call this midnight. It will take another circle around the Sun (another Mercury "year") before it is again pointing toward the Sun. This will be the next midday. In other words, one "day" on Mercury, from midday to midday, lasts two Mercury "years," or 176 Earth-days.

But on the dark, night side of Mercury, it is a different story. Places stay in the dark for 88 Earth days at a time. During this period, they lose most of their heat to space. Temperatures fall as low as −180°C. This is the same temperature as the planet Saturn, billions of miles away from the Sun.

Airless World

Because Mercury is such a small planet, it has only a weak gravitational pull, which means it has not been able to hold on to a thick atmosphere like Venus's or Earth's. In any case, such an atmosphere would have been driven off ages ago by the intense heat of the Sun.

Nevertheless, astronomers have detected very slight traces of gas around Mercury. This gas constitutes a very, very thin atmosphere. It contains hydrogen and helium gases that have come from the Sun and atoms of sodium that have come out of the baked rocks.

An Iron Planet

Mercury could be called the iron planet because it contains more iron for its size than any other planet. Its iron core makes up as much as four-fifths of the bulk of the planet. Only about one-fifth is rock.

This huge mass of iron makes Mercury magnetic, just as Earth's iron core makes it magnetic. But Mercury's magnetism is about 100 times weaker than Earth's, so it is doubtful whether you could use a magnetic compass to find your way around the planet, as you can on Earth.

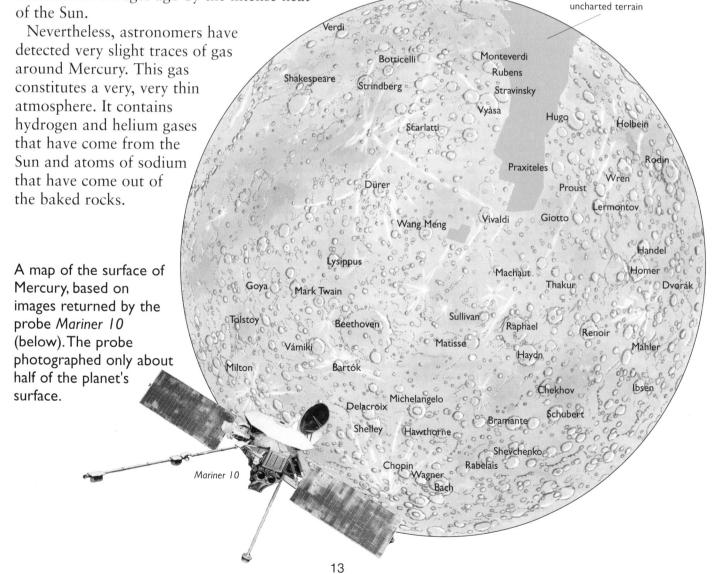

A map of the surface of Mercury, based on images returned by the probe *Mariner 10* (below). The probe photographed only about half of the planet's surface.

uncharted terrain

Mariner 10

Mercury Landscapes

When it flew past Mercury three times in 1974 and 1975, the space probe *Mariner 10* was able to take photographs of the planet. These pictures revealed that the half of Mercury that could be seen from *Mariner 10* is heavily cratered. There is no reason to think that the other half is any different.

At first sight, Mercury's surface looks like that of the Moon. But it doesn't have any large plains, or seas, as the Moon has. The craters, however, are just like those on the Moon. There are thousands upon thousands of them, ranging in size from shallow pits a few hundred feet across to large structures hundreds of miles in diameter. The large craters have raised walls, deep floors, and central mountain peaks.

The largest crater, named Beethoven, measures more than 400 miles (600 km) across, twice as big as the craters Shakespeare and Goethe. Most of the craters on Mercury are named after people famous in the arts, such as composers (Beethoven), playwrights (Shakespeare), poets (Goethe), and painters.

As mentioned already, there are no large plains, or seas, on Mercury, but there are smaller flat regions between many of the heavily cratered areas. These are known as intercrater plains.

Under Attack

Most of the craters on Mercury were created when it was bombarded by meteorites, or rocks from outer space. This happened mostly between about 4 and 4.5 billion years ago, not long after the planet formed.

Most of Mercury's craters date from this time. Many have since been flooded with lava, leaving them with flat, smooth floors. Some craters are much younger. Bright lines lead out from them like rays from the Sun. That is why these lines are called crater rays. They are lines of shiny material thrown out when the craters were formed.

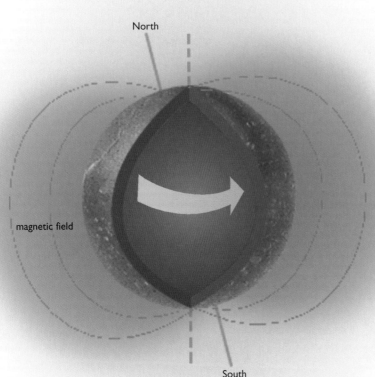

North

magnetic field

South

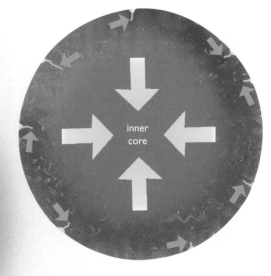

inner core

Mercury's huge iron core has had an enormous effect on the planet. It created a magnetic field (left). When the core shrunk a long-time ago, it caused the surface rocks to crack and pile up, creating steep cliffs.

Above: Craters and cliffs scar Mercury's surface.

Left: Rings of mountains surround Mercury's Caloris Basin.

The Big Basin

Sometime after the main meteor bombardment of Mercury ceased, the planet was struck by a massive asteroid. It created a huge crater, over 800 miles (1,300 km) across. The force of impact melted the surface rocks, which flooded the crater with lava. The impact also sent out shock waves, which rippled across the surface and threw up the rocks into circular mountain ranges, a mile or so high.

This huge, mountain-ringed formation is called the Caloris Basin. It was named Caloris (meaning heat) because it lies close to one of the hottest spots on the planet.

VEILED VENUS

Venus comes closer to Earth than any other planet. It looks beautiful when it hangs in the sky as an evening star, and the Romans named it after their goddess of beauty and love. But up close, Venus is far from beautiful. It has a suffocating, crushing atmosphere with acid clouds.

Venus is the easiest of the planets to spot in the sky. For several months each year, it can be seen in the darkening western sky just after sunset. That is why it is often referred to as the evening star. It comes out long before the real stars.

At other times of the year, early risers can spot Venus in the brightening eastern sky just before sunrise. All the real stars set long before it.

Venus appears so bright for two reasons. One, it comes closer to Earth than any other planet. And two, it is permanently covered in clouds, which reflect sunlight well.

Like Mercury, Venus appears to change size over time. This happens as it makes its orbit around the Sun. It looks smallest when it lies on the other

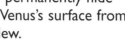

Thick clouds permanently hide Venus's surface from view.

side of the Sun viewed from Earth, and looks largest when it comes between the Sun and Earth. The shape of Venus also appears to change as it circles in its orbit. These changing shapes are its phases (see page 18).

Again like Mercury, Venus's orbit sometimes takes it in a path so that it appears to travel across the surface of the Sun. This event is known as the transit of Venus. Such transits are very rare. The last one took place in 1882, and the next will not take place until 2004.

At its closest, Venus is only about 26 million miles (42 million km) away from Earth. There are telescopes powerful enough to allow us to see features on Venus's surface. Even so, we are unable to because of the thick clouds that cover the planet.

Astronomers therefore use radar to study the surface. Radar uses beams of radio waves, which pass easily through clouds. Radar space probes, such as Magellan, beam down radio waves and pick up the reflections, or echoes. From the pattern of echoes, a detailed picture of the surface can be constructed.

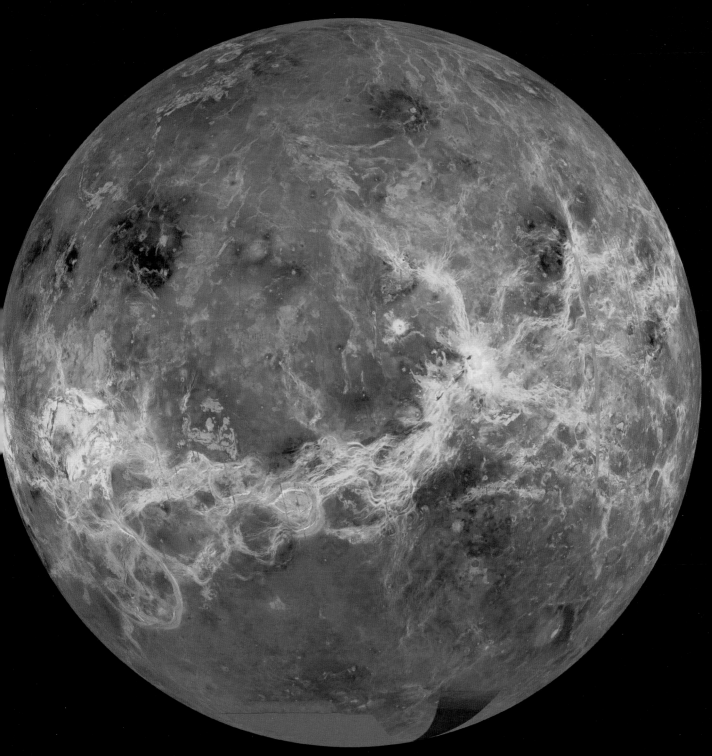

The Magellan probe used radar to peer through Venus's cloudy atmosphere. It spied a hot, dry, and barren landscape, dominated by volcanoes and the vast flows of lava that poured out of them.

Looking at Venus

Venus is sometimes called Earth's twin. Early in the 19th century, people thought that Venus might be a habitable world, similar to Earth but probably hotter. They imagined the planet covered with steamy swamps and populated by the kind of creatures that lived in the steamy swamps of Earth hundreds of millions of years ago.

But close examination by space probes have shown that Venus and Earth have little in common except their size. They have vastly different temperatures, atmospheres, and surfaces.

Slow Spinner

Venus orbits the Sun in almost a perfect circle, unlike Mercury, which follows an oval path around the Sun. It takes the planet 225 Earth-days to circle round the Sun once—this is Venus's "year."

Like all planets, Venus spins on its axis as it travels in its orbit around the Sun. But it does so very slowly—slower, in fact, than any other planet. It takes 243 Earth-days to

VENUS DATA

Diameter: 7,521 miles (12,104 km)
Average distance from Sun: 67,000,000 miles (108,000,000 km)
Mass (Earth=1): 0.8
Density (water=1): 5.2
Spins on axis in: 243 days
Circles round Sun in: 225 days
Number of moons: 0

spin around once. It spins around in the opposite direction to the other planets. They rotate from west to east, but Venus spins from east to west. If you lived on Venus, you would see the Sun rise in the west and set in the east—the exact opposite of what happens on Earth.

Below: The different phases of Venus. The size and shape of the planet we see changes as it moves closer or farther away from Earth. It is smallest when it is "full" (full circle).

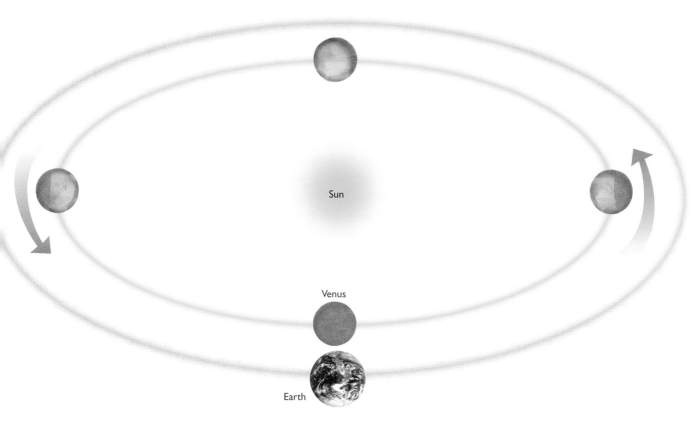

Crushing Pressure

However, if you did live on Venus, you would probably never be able to see the Sun rise and set. This is because the planet is always covered by thick white clouds that move rapidly through the atmosphere.

Venus has a very thick (dense) atmosphere—much thicker than Earth's atmosphere. The pressure (force) of the atmosphere at ground level on Venus is about 90 times greater than it is on Earth. Without some sort of suit or equipment that would make an adjustment to the pressure, a visitor to Venus would be crushed to death.

The main reason why Venus has such a thick and heavy atmosphere is because the atmosphere is made up almost entirely of carbon dioxide. Carbon dioxide is much heavier than the main two gases in Earth's atmosphere—nitrogen and oxygen.

Venus's atmosphere also contains traces of

Above: From Earth, we see different amounts of Venus lit up by the Sun as it travels in its orbit. In other words, it shows phases, like the moon does.

water vapor (water in the form of a gas) and poisonous gases, such as sulfur dioxide and hydrogen chloride. All these gases, along with the carbon dioxide, have been spewed out by the many volcanoes that have erupted on Venus over the years.

Below: The most of Venus's very dense (thick) atmosphere consists of carbon dioxide.

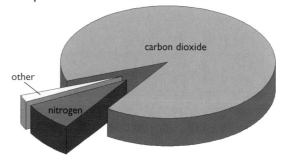

Top Temperature

Venus is about 25 million miles (40 million km) closer to the Sun than is Earth, which means it is extremely warm. Space probes have found that temperatures on the planet can reach as high as 480°C—hotter even than on Mercury. While Mercury is hot on one side and cold on the other, Venus is hot all over.

Like a Greenhouse

Venus stays so hot because its thick atmosphere traps or holds in heat, much like a garden greenhouse does. This is called the "greenhouse effect."

The planet is heated by sunlight, which passes through the atmosphere and heats the surface. The surface warms up and gives off heat rays. But the atmosphere prevents rays from escaping into space. They are absorbed by the carbon dioxide, water vapor, and other gases. Because the heat cannot escape, it builds up, making Venus the hottest planet in the solar system.

Acid Clouds

Venus would be even hotter if it were not for the haze and clouds in the atmosphere. On Earth, clouds are made up of tiny droplets of water or ice crystals. On Venus, however, they are made up of droplets of sulfuric acid. This is the kind of acid found in car batteries.

These acid clouds formed from the sulfur dioxide gas given off by the eruption of Venus's volcanoes. In the atmosphere, under the action of sunlight, the sulfur dioxide combines with water vapor to form the acid.

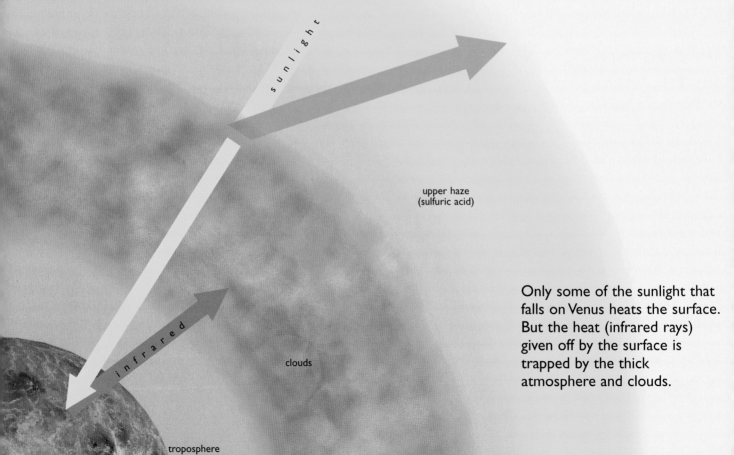

sunlight

infrared

upper haze
(sulfuric acid)

clouds

troposphere

Only some of the sunlight that falls on Venus heats the surface. But the heat (infrared rays) given off by the surface is trapped by the thick atmosphere and clouds.

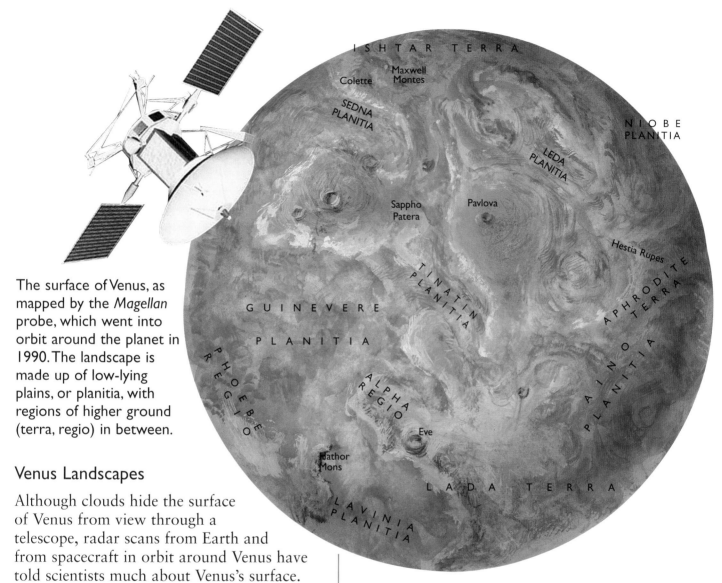

The surface of Venus, as mapped by the *Magellan* probe, which went into orbit around the planet in 1990. The landscape is made up of low-lying plains, or planitia, with regions of higher ground (terra, regio) in between.

Venus Landscapes

Although clouds hide the surface of Venus from view through a telescope, radar scans from Earth and from spacecraft in orbit around Venus have told scientists much about Venus's surface.

Low, rolling plains cover about two-thirds of the surface of Venus. They have been likened to Earth's ocean basins. Venus has just two main upland areas, similar to Earth's continents.

The largest continent lies close to Venus's equator. It is named Aphrodite Terra—Aphrodite being the Greek name for the goddess of love and beauty, and Terra meaning "earth" or "land." This continent stretches for about 6,000 miles (9,500 km) and covers an area about the size of Africa.

It is cleft by deep valleys, known as chasma. Deepest is Diana Chasma, which is more than 2.5 miles (4 km) deep and nearly 200 miles (300 km) wide in places.

The other continent lies further north. It is named Ishtar Terra, after the Babylonian goddess of love. It is about the same size as the United States. This continent is noted for its lofty mountains, including Maxwell Montes. They rise to heights of more than 5 miles (8 km)—about the same height as Earth's highest mountain, Mount Everest.

Venus's Volcanoes

Venus is covered with thousands of volcanoes. They have erupted all over the planet for millions of years, helping form its characteristic flat, rolling landscape. Many of them may still be active.

Most of the volcanoes found on Venus are the type known on Earth as shield volcanoes. The volcanoes on the Hawaiian islands, for example, are this type. Shield volcanoes are noted for their runny lava, which can travel a very long way. Venus's vast plains have been created by long and repeated lava flows.

Pancakes and Spiders

Volcanic activity on Venus has also produced features that can be found nowhere else in the solar system. They include flat circular domes, which look rather like pancakes. They are typically around 15 miles (25 km) across. Astronomers think that the pancakes formed when thick lava bubbled up through cracks in the surface. This lava did not flow far because it was so viscous (sticky).

There are other strange formations on Venus that look like spiders' webs. They are called "arachnoids," after a word that means "spider." Arachnoids have a central crater surrounded by a network of fine lines. These appear to be fractures (cracks) in the surface, made by molten rock pushing up from below.

Coronae (meaning "crowns") are other volcanic features unique to Venus. They are circular structures surrounded by many ridges and valleys and networks of fractures.

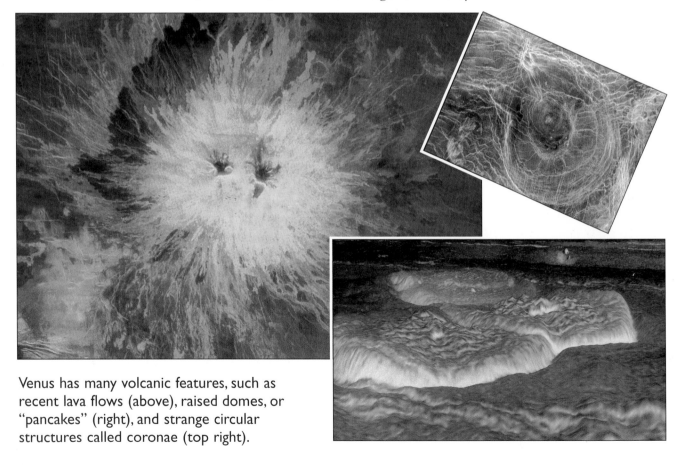

Venus has many volcanic features, such as recent lava flows (above), raised domes, or "pancakes" (right), and strange circular structures called coronae (top right).

Venus's Craters

Like all the inner planets, Venus was bombarded heavily by meteorites soon after it formed. They would have dug out craters, like those we see on Mercury today. But since then Venus's volcanoes have been at work, constantly pouring out lava that has filled in the ancient craters.

Today, the relatively few craters that can be seen on Venus are all quite young. They show up clearly against the older lava plains. There are some really spectacular craters, some more than 150 miles (250 km) across. In pictures, we see them surrounded by fresh material dug out when meteorites smashed into the surface.

The atmosphere helps protect Venus from smaller meteorites. They burn up like meteors or break apart when they hit the atmosphere. Sometimes we see craters with several pits inside them, showing where separate pieces of meteorite have landed. This kind of crater is not found on Mercury or the Moon because they have no atmosphere to break up the incoming missiles.

Below: Volcanoes by the hundreds dot Venus's surface. Many are probably still active.
Bottom: Only a few impact craters are found on Venus. This one measures about 30 miles (50 km) across.

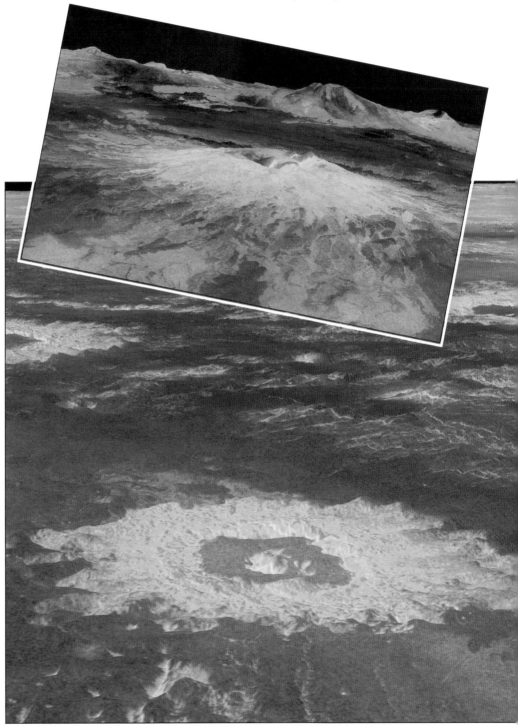

PLANET EARTH

Our home planet, Earth, is the largest of the inner planets, but it is a dwarf compared with the giant outer planets, such as Jupiter. It behaves like a typical planet, spinning around on its axis as it orbits the Sun. What makes Earth unique among planets is that it teems with life.

Earth provides a comfortable home for millions of different species (kinds) of living things, from tiny microscopic plants to gigantic animals, such as whales. Whales are the biggest animals that have ever lived, bigger even than the dinosaurs. They are masters of their environment—the oceans— where life is believed to have started billions of years ago.

Why is there so much life on Earth but none on the other planets? The answer seems to be that Earth just happens to be located in the right place in the solar system and just happens to be the right size.

Earth is located in the solar system in what is sometimes called the life zone. It receives just the right amounts of heat and light from the Sun to provide just the right conditions for life to flourish. In particular, its location allows water to exist as a liquid, and water is needed by almost all living things.

Earth has the right size and make-up to take advantage of conditions in the life zone. They give it a large enough mass and gravitational pull to hold onto a layer of gases, or atmosphere. The atmosphere provides oxygen for living things to breathe. It also acts like a blanket to help keep Earth warm, and to shield it against deadly radiation from space.

Earth is often called a living planet for another reason. Like a living thing, it is constantly changing. On its outside, the weather, running water, and other forces are continually wearing away and reshaping Earth's surface. Beneath the surface, on the inside, movements in the rocks cause the continents to move, volcanoes to erupt, and earthquakes to take place.

Left: This is a volcanic rock called pumice, which is widely found on Earth. It formed from lava that poured out of ancient volcanoes.

A view of our very watery planet Earth, showing the vast Pacific Ocean and the continents of North and South America.

Looking at Earth

Earth is the third planet out from the Sun, located between Venus and Mars. Like these and all the other planets, Earth has two motions in space. It both spins around—rotates—on its axis and it circles around the Sun.

We do not feel the Earth move, of course, because we are moving with it. But it moves very, very fast. A person standing on the Equator, is traveling around the center of the Earth at a speed of 1,000 mph (1,600 km/h). At the same time, the inhabitants of Earth are hurtling through space in orbit around the Sun at a speed of more than 66,000 mph (105,000 km/h).

Marking Time

Because Earth rotates, the Sun and the other stars seem to circle around Earth. This is why our early ancestors thought that Earth was the center of the universe.

Every day at noon, the Sun reaches its highest point in the sky. The time between two noons is always 24 hours, or 1 day. The day is one of our basic units of time.

EARTH DATA

Diameter: 7,927 miles (12,756 km)
Average distance from Sun: 93,000,000 miles (150,000,000 km)
Mass (Earth=1): 1
Density (water=1): 5.5
Spins on axis in: 23.94 hours
Circles round Sun in: 365.25 days
Number of moons: 1

Just as Earth always spins completely around in the same period of time, so Earth always takes the same time to complete its orbit around the Sun—a little over 365 days. This period is our other basic unit of time, the year.

The Tilting Earth

Earth does not spin in an upright position as it travels in its orbit around the Sun. Its

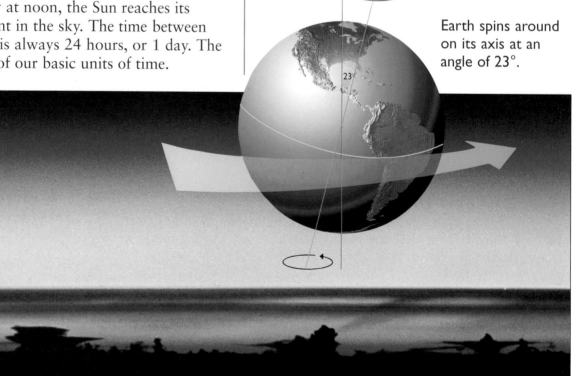

Earth spins around on its axis at an angle of 23°.

axis is slightly tilted (by 23½ degrees). Earth always stays tilted in the same direction in space. This means that places on Earth are tilted more toward the Sun— and are hotter—at some times of the year than at others.

As a result, most places experience regular changes in temperature and the weather throughout the course of the year, bringing about what we call the seasons. In many parts of the world, there are four seasons— spring, summer, fall (autumn), and winter. Mars also has seasons.

The Atmosphere

By weather, we mean the state of the atmosphere—whether it is hot or cold, dry or wet, still or windy, clear or cloudy. The atmosphere is the layer of air that surrounds Earth. It is thickest (densest) near the ground in a layer called the troposphere by meteorologists, the scientists who study the weather.

Above the troposphere are other layers, called the stratosphere, mesosphere, thermosphere, and exosphere. Going up through these layers, the air gets thinner and thinner until it merges into space at a height of about 300 miles (500 km).

Left: A view of our atmosphere from space, taken by orbiting astronauts. The blueness is caused by the air particles scattering the sunlight. Compared with the size of Earth, the atmosphere is thinner than the peel is to the size of an orange.

Right: Earth's atmosphere extends up for more than 300 miles (500 km), where it merges into space. Some spacecraft orbit at the edge of the atmosphere. Glowing lights called the aurora occur high up too. Meteors burn up lower down.

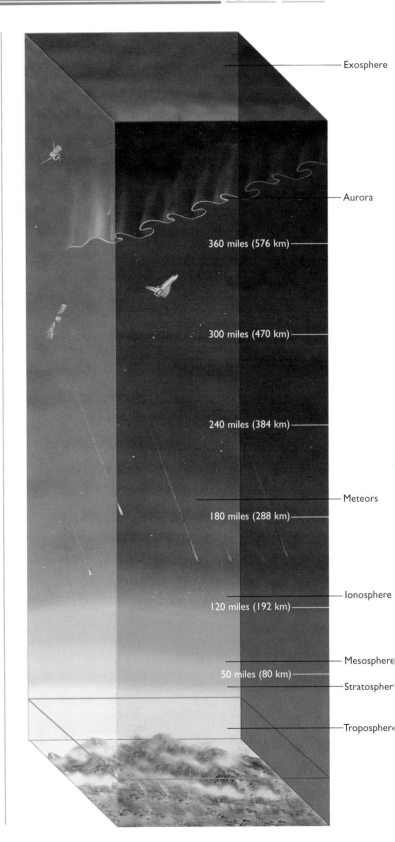

Exosphere

Aurora

360 miles (576 km)

300 miles (470 km)

240 miles (384 km)

Meteors

180 miles (288 km)

Ionosphere

120 miles (192 km)

Mesosphere

50 miles (80 km)

Stratosphere

Troposphere

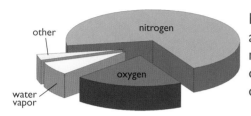

other
nitrogen
oxygen
water vapor

Earth's atmosphere is made up mostly of nitrogen and oxygen.

Gases in the Atmosphere

The two main gases in Earth's atmosphere are nitrogen (about 78 percent) and oxygen (about 21 percent). Oxygen is by far the most important of the two, because it is the gas humans and almost all living things must breathe to stay alive.

There are traces of many other gases in the atmosphere. One is carbon dioxide, the gas that humans breathe out. It plays an important part in life on Earth because plants need to take it in to make food. In sunlight, they combine carbon dioxide with water to make sugar, their food. This process is called photosynthesis, which means literally "to make light."

Another important trace gas in the atmosphere is water vapor—water in the form of a gas. Water plays a vital part in our weather. Water circulates constantly between Earth's surface and atmosphere. This is called the water cycle.

Most water gets into the air through evaporation, which is when the heat of the Sun turns surface water, such as in oceans or lakes, to vapor. In the air, the vapor cools and turns into droplets of water or ice crystals, creating mists, clouds, rain, and snow.

Water is found nearly everywhere on Earth—in the ground, on the surface, and in the atmosphere. In the atmosphere, water is found as vapor (gas) and as tiny droplets in clouds. When the droplets get big enough, they fall to the ground as rain. Vapor, clouds, and rain are features of Earth's never-ending water cycle.

Land and Sea

Earth has quite a different surface from all the other planets. Large areas of its rocky crust (outer layer) are hidden under water, which forms vast oceans. The oceans cover more than 70 percent of Earth's surface, more than twice the area of the dry land. The Pacific Ocean alone covers an area equal to that of all the land masses put together.

The main land masses are the seven continents: North America, South America, Europe, Asia, Africa, Australia, and Antarctica. Earth's crust is thickest under the continents, averaging about 25 miles (40 km) in thickness. The crust under the oceans is much thinner—only about 6 miles (10 km).

Drifting Continents

The map shows the location and shapes of the continents as we know them today. But they have not always looked like this. About 200 million years ago, all these land masses were joined together to form one supercontinent, which geologists call Pangaea.

Since then, they have split apart and drifted across the face of the Earth to where they are located today. They will continue to drift in the future, so that in many millions of years' time, the arrangement of Earth's land masses will be quite different from what it is today.

How does this continental drift occur? It happens because Earth's crust is not a single layer of rock but is made up of many sections, called plates. Each plate is able to move. The continents sit on plates and move with them. This theory of moving plates is known as plate tectonics.

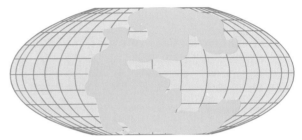

170 million years ago

50 million years ago

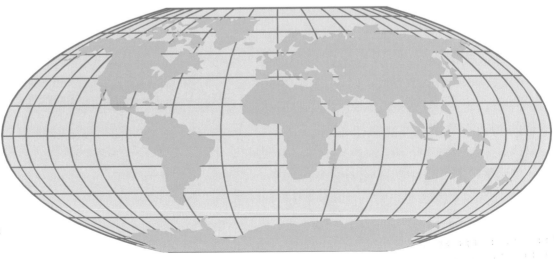

Right: Earth's surface as it is today, made up of continents and islands set in a vast saltwater ocean. But the Earth has not always looked like this. It has changed drastically over the last 150 million years, and is changing still.

Wandering Plates

The rocks that form the plates of Earth's crust are hard and rigid. But beneath the crust, the rocks are much hotter and softer and can flow slowly, something like chewing gum or putty. Heat from inside the Earth sets up currents in these rocks, and it is these that carry the plates along.

The plates fit together something like a jigsaw puzzle. Where they meet can be the site of all kinds of unusual geological events. Two great plates meet in the middle of the South Atlantic Ocean, for example. They are pulling apart, causing the ocean to grow wider. This also happens in Earth's other oceans and is called sea-floor spreading.

In other parts of the world, plates are colliding. This is happening, for example, off the west coast of South America. An ocean plate is pushing against the plate carrying South America. Something has to give, and land at the edge of South America rides up. This is what created the great mountain range known as the Andes.

Volcanoes and Earthquakes

At the same time, the ocean plate dips down under the land plate. As it does so, it rubs against the surrounding rocks. This can make the ground shake—an earthquake. The friction also makes the plate material heat up and melt.

Pressure forces the molten rock upward through cracks to the surface. This is what volcanoes are and explains why there are so many volcanoes in the Andes.

Volcanoes or earthquakes or both occur at most of the other places in the world where plates meet. The most active regions for volcanoes are around the outer rim of the Pacific Ocean, where plates collide head-on. Some 300 volcanoes are found in the so-called Ring of Fire.

Slow-moving currents in the rocks deep underground carry along plates of Earth's crust. Under the oceans, plates are moving apart, causing them to widen. Where ocean plates come up against plates carrying the continents, the land rides up, creating mountains.

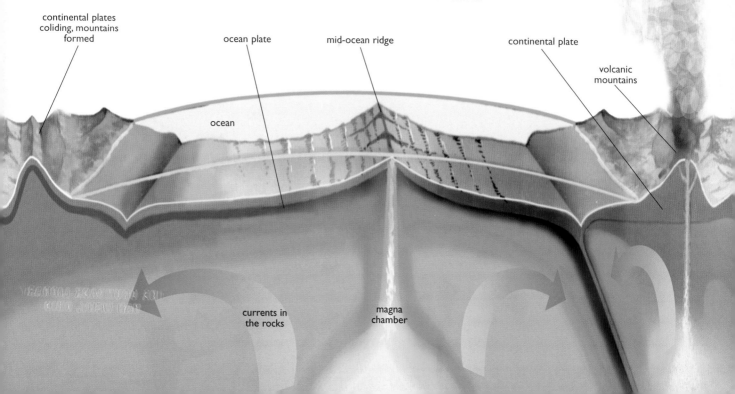

continental plates
coliding, mountains
formed

ocean plate

mid-ocean ridge

continental plate

volcanic
mountains

ocean

currents in
the rocks

magna
chamber

Under the Weather

Volcanoes and earthquakes are not the only things that help reshape the Earth's surface. The weather and the flow of water contribute as well. They cause the surface gradually to erode, or wear away. Flowing water is one of the primary agents of erosion. Rivers cut deep into rock to create such natural wonders as the Grand Canyon.

Water carries away the material it gouges out of rock and deposits it elsewhere as sediment. Over millions of years, sediment can build up and turn into rock. Most of the rocks that cover our Earth now are sedimentary rocks, which formed from deposits laid down in ancient seas.

On the other planets, all the rocks are volcanic, meaning that they formed from molten rock. However, Mars may be an exception. Recent evidence shows that water did once flow on the planet, so there may well be sedimentary rocks there, too.

Above: An Hawaiian volcano erupts in a spectacular fireworks display.

Below: The Grand Canyon has been worn away by the Colorado River over millions of years.

THE RED PLANET

Mars shines in the night sky with a fiery reddish-orange color. The color reminded the ancient Romans of fire and blood, so they named Mars after their god of war. People once thought that there might be life on Mars—even intelligent life. But space probes have found no signs of it.

Mars comes nearer to Earth than any other planet except Venus. It is most visible in the night sky about every 26 months. That is when it comes closest to Earth as the two planets orbit the Sun. Astronomers call these times oppositions.

Every 15 years or so, Mars gets especially close to Earth, coming within about 35 million miles (56 million km). Then it becomes one of the brightest objects in the night sky rivaling even Jupiter in brightness. It is easy to tell which planet is which, however, because Mars is reddish and Jupiter is pure white.

Through a telescope, astronomers can see some details on Mars's surface. There are dark markings, which seem to change shape over time. And there are white regions at the north and south poles. They look like the areas of ice found at Earth's North and South Poles.

Mars is also similar to Earth in other ways. It completes its rotation on its axis in a little more than 24½ hours. In other words, its "day" is only about ½ hour longer than our own.

Also, Mars has seasons like Earth does. As on Earth, the seasons are caused by the tilt of the planet's axis in space. This tilt means that parts of Mars are closer to the Sun at some times than at others. Those that are tilted most toward the Sun enjoy their warmest season—summer. When they are tilted farthest away from the Sun, they experience their coldest season—winter.

On Mars, the seasons are nearly twice as long as they are on Earth because Mars's "year" (the time it takes to circle the Sun) is nearly twice as long as our year. Because Mars is so much farther from the Sun than Earth is, temperatures during their seasons are much colder than they are on Earth.

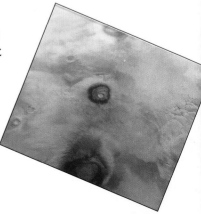

Mars boasts massive volcanoes bigger than Mount Everest. Ancient lava flows cover much of the northern hemisphere (half) of Mars.

The red planet Mars, looks reddish in the night sky and also up close. Like Earth, it has ice caps and clouds in its thin atmosphere.

Mars's Atmosphere

Mars is similar to Earth in one other way—it has an atmosphere. This can be told from Earth because at times astronomers cannot see any markings on Mars through their telescopes. The markings have been blotted out by huge dust storms that sweep over the whole planet. Without an atmosphere, there would not be any dust storms.

Mars's atmosphere, however, is nothing like Earth's. There is very little of it—scientists say that it is very thin. It presses down on the surface with only one percent of the pressure (force) of Earth's atmosphere.

Even though its atmosphere is very thin, strong winds sometimes blow on Mars. This is what whips up dust from the surface and creates planet-wide dust storms. On occasions, winds may blow at speeds of 200 mph (300 km/h) or more—these are the speeds winds reach in tornadoes on Earth.

Gases in the Atmosphere

The atmosphere on Mars also has a much different chemical make-up than Earth's. It is made up mainly of carbon dioxide, which is the gas given off by the burning of fuels such as oil. The carbon dioxide on Mars, of course, did not come from burning fuels—it was given off when volcanoes erupted on the planet.

Mars's atmosphere consists mainly of carbon dioxide.

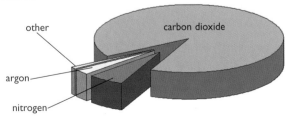

other
carbon dioxide
argon
nitrogen

MARS DATA

Diameter: 4,221 miles (6,792 km)

Average distance from Sun: 142,000,000 miles (228,000,000 km)

Mass (Earth=1): 0.1

Density (water=1): 3.9

Spins on axis in: 24.63 hours

Circles round Sun in: 687 days

Number of moons: 2

There are also tiny amounts of other gases in Mars's atmosphere, including nitrogen and oxygen. These are the two gases that make up our own atmosphere. But there is nowhere near enough oxygen for humans to breathe on Mars. An astronaut who explored Mars would have to wear a spacesuit with breathing apparatus that provided oxygen to breathe.

Cloudy Skies

Traces of yet another gas can be found in Mars's atmosphere—water vapor. This is water in the form of a gas. On Earth, the heat of the Sun turns water into vapor, which rises into the air. This process is called evaporation. There is no liquid water on Mars, but there is frozen water, or ice. The heat of the Sun turns this into vapor, which rises into the atmosphere.

On Earth, as water vapor rises, it gets colder, and it turns back into little droplets of water. These droplets group together to form white clouds. A similar thing happens on Mars, only the clouds that form are made up of tiny ice crystals, not water droplets, because the temperature is so low. Clouds can often be seen on Mars clinging to the sides of the tall volcanoes. And low clouds, or mists, often form in Mars's many valleys.

Above: Part of Mars's southern hemisphere. The circular white patch is a vast region covered in a water-ice mist.

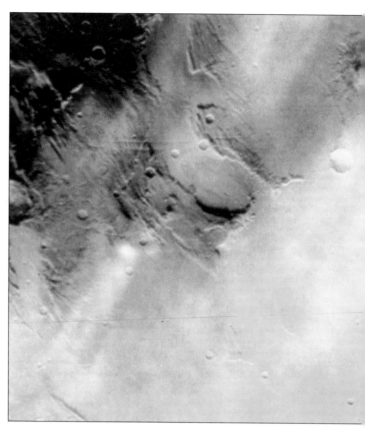

Above: Dust storms often blow up in the sandy desert regions of Mars (lower part of picture).

Sunset on Mars, snapped by one of the Viking landers, which landed on the Red Planet in 1976.

Above: The northern ice cap of Mars shows up in this picture taken by the Hubble Space Telescope.

Below: Much of Mars consists of sandy plains, strewn with rocks. This Viking picture shows Chryse, the Plain of Gold.

Temperatures on Mars

Mars is on average about 50 million miles (80 million km) further away from the Sun than Earth. This means that it is much colder than Earth.

On any planet, the hottest region is near its "waist," or equator. This is the part that receives the most heat from the Sun. Around Earth's equator, temperatures regularly rise to more than 104°F (40°C). But on Mars, temperatures at the equator struggle to rise above freezing point 32°F (0°C). But they may rise briefly to about room temperature 70°F (21°C) in midsummer.

Elsewhere on the planet, temperatures are low all the time. When the *Viking 1* probe landed on the Martian plain Chryse in 1976, it found that the temperature around midday was only about –20°F (–30°C). During the night, the temperature fell to below –110°F (–80°C). On Mars, the temperature falls rapidly after the Sun sets because the atmosphere is so thin. Earth's thick atmosphere acts like a blanket to help hold in the warmth of the day. The coolest

parts of Mars are the regions around the north and south poles. They are at their coldest in winter, when the tilt of Mars leaves them farthest away from the Sun. Then, temperatures drop to –240°F (–150°C) or below.

The Ice Caps

The main features of the polar regions of Mars are the ice caps, which can be seen through telescopes from Earth. They change size with the Martian seasons.

As to be expected, the ice caps are largest in winter, when the weather is intensely cold. As spring comes and the weather warms up, they start to melt and shrink in size. The caps are smallest in summer. Then, as autumn comes and temperatures begin to fall, ice freezes out of the atmosphere, and the caps start to grow again.

There is always some ice left at the poles even in midsummer. Astronomers believe that this is mainly water ice—frozen water. The icy material that makes the ice caps grow as winter comes is probably frozen carbon dioxide, or "dry ice."

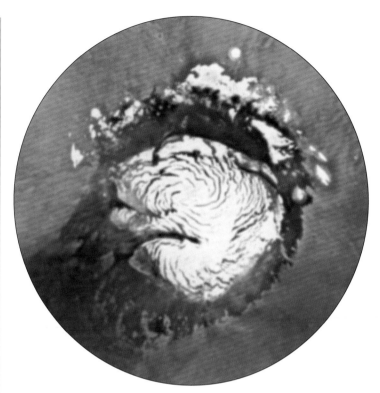

A close-up of Mars's north polar ice cap. In summer, the cap measures up to 370 miles (600 km) across and is mainly water ice. In winter, the cap expands as frozen carbon dioxide settles over it.

On the Plains of Gold

On June 19, 1976, the first of two identical Viking probes slipped into orbit around Mars. It had set off from Earth just 10 months before. *Viking I* then spent a month looking for a suitable landing site, and on July 20 it released a lander. Using the drag of the planet's atmosphere, rockets, and parachutes, the lander made a soft touchdown on a region of Mars known as Chryse Planitia—the Plains of Gold. Within seconds, its cameras began photographing the surrounding area. It looked like a stony desert on Earth, with many small rocks scattered around a sandy landscape. This was the first clear close-up view of another planet sent back to Earth. Soon the lander extended a meteorology (weather) boom and began sending back measurements of wind speed, atmospheric pressure, and temperature. The lander became Mars's first weather station.

Viking orbiter

Left: The two Viking craft (inset) that went into orbit around Mars in 1976 mapped the whole planet in considerable detail, much of it in color.

Opposite top: Much of Mars's southern hemisphere is covered with craters, large and small.

Looking at the Landscape

The surface of Mars boasts all kinds of fascinating features—vast deserts, gigantic volcanoes, long valleys, huge basins, and craters large and small.

Like all the inner planets, Mars was bombarded by huge lumps of rock—meteorites—early in its history. This bombardment scarred the planet with pits, or craters. Much of the southern hemisphere (half) of the planet is still dotted with ancient craters. They make this region of Mars look rather like the highland regions of the Moon.

The craters on Mars look much like those on the Moon. They have raised walls and low floors. The larger ones have a small mountain range in the center. In some, the impact (blow) that formed the crater melted the rocks. Molten material flowed into the surrounding area, forming a noticeable ring around the crater. This kind of thing never happened on the Moon.

The Basins

Two very large meteorites or asteroids hit the southern hemisphere of Mars long ago, gouging out two huge basins. They are both surrounded by low mountain ranges, thrown up by the force of the impacts.

The largest basin, named Hellas, is more than 1,350 miles (2,200 km) across. The floor of the basin is flat and resembles a sandy desert on Earth. The other basin, Argyre, is only about half the size of Hellas. Argyre becomes very conspicuous at times when it fills with frost.

The floor of the gigantic Hellas basin. It is the lowest region on Mars, about 2 miles (3 km) lower than the surrounding surface.

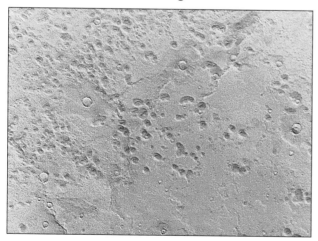

The Volcanoes

The heavily cratered region of the southern hemisphere of Mars extends some way into the northern hemisphere. But vast plains cover most of the north. They were created by the lava flows from innumerable volcanoes.

The greatest of these volcanoes are found just north of Mars's equator, on a huge bulge on the surface in a region astronomers call Tharsis. There are four major volcanoes. The biggest of them all is Olympus Mons (Mount Olympus).

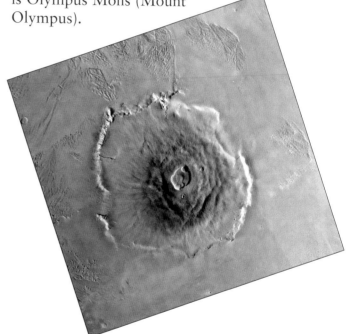

The biggest volcano we know in the solar system, Mars's Olympus Mons. Its central crater is over 40 miles (70 km) across.

This gigantic mountain soars to a height of around 17 miles (27 km). This is four times the height of the highest peak in North America, Denali (Mt. McKinley) in Alaska. Olympus Mons is very broad at the base, measuring more than 400 miles (640 km) across. It is a type of volcano called a shield volcano, like those on Hawaii such as Mauna Loa.

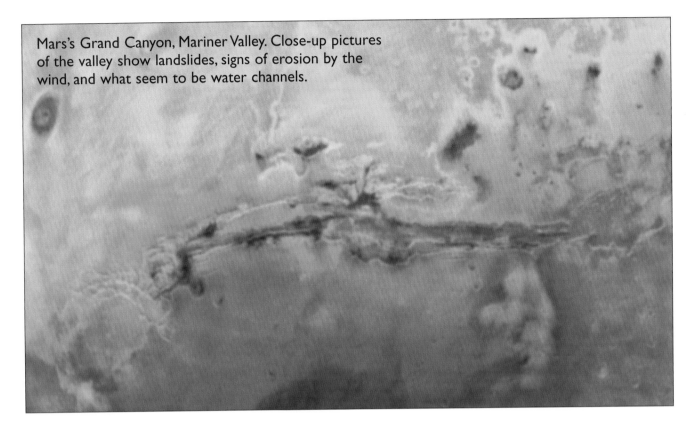

Mars's Grand Canyon, Mariner Valley. Close-up pictures of the valley show landslides, signs of erosion by the wind, and what seem to be water channels.

Canyonlands

Just to the east of the Tharsis Bulge is the biggest natural feature on Mars, a huge valley that runs close to the equator for more than 2,500 miles (4,000 km). It is called Mariner Valley (Valles Marineris), after the Mariner space probe that discovered it.

The main part of the valley is up to 250 miles (400 km) wide and 6 miles (10 km) deep. It has many side branches that end in steep-sided canyons. It has often been called Mars's Grand Canyon, after the spectacular natural feature of that name in Arizona. But it is four times deeper, six times wider, and ten times longer than the Grand Canyon on Earth.

The only comparable valley on Earth is the Great Rift Valley in East Africa, which formed when two blocks of the Earth's surface moved apart. Mariner Valley probably formed in a similar way, when theMartian surface cracked. Maybe it split apart when the Tharsis Bulge forced its way up.

Mariner Valley certainly did not form as the Grand Canyon did. The Grand Canyon was formed over many millions of years as a result of the Colorado River cutting through the surface rocks. Mariner Valley does, however, show signs that water has flowed through the canyons and gorges at some time in the past.

Sandblasting

The surface of Mars has been shaped mainly by volcanoes, internal forces, and meteorites. But other forces have also been at work—in particular, the wind. In Mars's desert regions, the wind creates rippling dunes—waves in the sandy soil.

The strong winds on Mars also whip up sand and dust from the surface. They "sandblast" the mountains, craters, and other landforms, slowly wearing them down. Such wearing away, or erosion, is common in desert regions on Earth.

Most erosion on Earth is caused by flowing water, however. There are signs that flowing water has also caused some erosion on Mars.

The Channels

Mariner Valley and the large canyons on Mars were formed by massive movements in the planet's crust. But most of the smaller valleys and channels that snake over the surface of Mars were obviously formed in a different way. Some were made by lava flowing from ancient volcanoes. Similar channels are found on the Moon—a classic example is Alpine Valley, which cuts through the lunar Alps.

But many channels look as though they have been made by flowing water. Some look like dried-up riverbeds. They display the typical features of river formation— starting out narrow (where the river rises), then gradually broadening out and splitting

into branches (tributaries) downstream. Other channels start broad, as if created in massive floods. Elsewhere, we find teardrop-shaped patterns around craters, which look as if they have been made by rivers flowing round them.

Water Everywhere

Astronomers are now almost certain that the most of the channels they have spotted on Mars were made by flowing water long ago. They think that the vast desert plains of northern Mars once might even have been oceans.

This supports the idea that Mars once had a warmer climate and a thicker atmosphere. This would have been long ago, when volcanic eruptions were taking place all over the planet. But over time, the climate cooled and the atmosphere slowly escaped into space, taking with it most of the planet's moisture.

The moisture that remains on Mars today is in the form of ice at the poles and clouds, mists, and frost elsewhere. Many astronomers now believe that there is a lot of moisture on Mars that has not yet been detected. Most likely, it is trapped as ice beneath the surface. A similar thing happens in Earth tundra regions, which are the cold land areas near the North and South poles. There, ground below the surface stays permanently frozen—it is known as permafrost.

Permafrost may well be found all over Mars. If so, it will provide a much needed supply of water when the human exploration of the Red Planet begins later in the 21st century.

Left: A region of Mars known as Mangala Vallis, showing the boundary between higher, older crust and a smooth plain. The deep channels seen here were probably cut by flowing water.

Fear and Terror

Mars has two tiny satellites, or moons, which U.S. astronomer Asaph Hall discovered in 1877. They are named Phobos (meaning "fear") and Deimos ("terror"). They are not large bodies like our own Moon, but are tiny lumps of rock, shaped rather like a potato. Phobos, the largest, measures less than 20 miles (30 km) long—about twice as long as Deimos. They are both scarred with craters and fault lines where the surface has cracked.

Phobos and Deimos are almost certainly not true moons, in the sense of having been formed along with Mars when the planets were born. Probably they were once two of the rocky lumps we call asteroids. Most asteroids circle in a broad band, or belt, between the orbits of Mars and Jupiter. But some have orbits that take them outside this

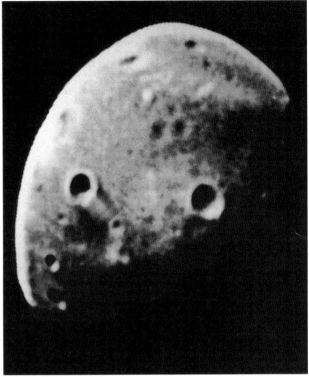

Above: Deimos, the smaller of the two Martian moons, is relatively smooth and is strewn with boulders.

Left: Phobos is more heavily cratered, and its surface looks rather like the rugged highland regions of the Moon.

belt. Long ago, two of these asteroids passed close to Mars and were captured by its gravity, becoming the moons of Mars we find today.

Phobos orbits Mars very fast and low. It travels only about 5,800 miles (9,300 km) above the surface. This is lower than any other moon in the solar system. It orbits Mars in less than 8 hours. If you lived on the planet, you would see Phobos streak across the sky at night, traveling from west to east. It would look nearly as bright as Venus looks from Earth. Deimos circles more than twice as far away and would look just like a star in the sky.

Life on Mars

In the 19th century many astronomers and ordinary people believed that there must be life on Mars. They saw that it had certain things in common with Earth, such as seasons, ice caps, and the length of its day. In 1877, an Italian astronomer named Giovanni Schiaparelli reported seeing what he thought might be canals on Mars. He really meant natural channels, but others thought he meant proper canals—artificially constructed waterways. (Humans themselves were building canals on a large scale by then.)

Other astronomers also used telescopes to detect what they thought were canals on Mars. Among them was U.S. astronomer Percival Lowell. He pictured an intelligent race of Martians digging canals to channel water from the poles to warmer regions near the equator so that they could grow crops.

Many astronomers, though, saw no canals, which is not surprising because there are not any on Mars. Nevertheless

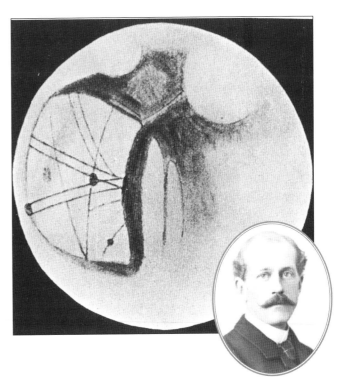

US astronomer Percival Lowell (1855–1916) was convinced that there was life on Mars. He built the famous Lowell Observatory at Flagstaff, Arizona, to study the Red Planet and made drawings of networks of "canals" on the surface.

some people still expected to learn of some traces of life, or at least canals, when the first space probes flew past Mars in the 1960s. They were disappointed—Mars turned out to be a cold and barren wilderness, unsuitable for life as we know it.

Later investigations have confirmed that it is most unlikely that even primitive forms of life can exist on Mars today. However, it appears that Mars had a warmer and wetter climate in the past. It is possible that some life forms may have developed then. Maybe their remains, or fossils, are waiting to be discovered on this fascinating Red Planet.

A meteorite from Mars, ALH84001. In 1996, NASA scientists theoriaed that it contained fossils of primitive Martian life forms. This was later disproved.

Glossary

ASTEROIDS Small lumps of rock or metal that circle the Sun. Most circle in a broad band (the asteroid belt) between the orbits of Mars and Jupiter.

ATMOSPHERE The layer of gases around Earth or another heavenly body.

CHASMA A deep valley.

COMET A small icy lump that gives off clouds of gas and dust and starts to shine when it gets near the Sun.

CONTINENTAL DRIFT The gradual movement of the continents across the Earth.

CORE The center part of a body.

CRATER A circular pit in the surface of a planet or moon.

CRUST The hard outer layer of a planet or a moon.

ELLIPTICAL Having the shape of an ellipse; an oval shape.

EROSION The gradual wearing away of the landscape by flowing water, the weather, wind, and so on.

EVENING STAR Usually the planet Venus appearing in the western sky just after sunset. Mercury can be an evening star, too.

FALLING STAR A popular name for a meteor.

FAULT A crack in the surface of a planet or moon caused by massive movements in the rocks.

GALAXY A "star island" in space. Our own galaxy is called the Milky Way.

GRAVITY The pull, or force of attraction, that every body has because of its mass.

GREENHOUSE EFFECT When the atmosphere of a planet traps heat like a greenhouse.

HEAVENS The night sky; the heavenly bodies are the objects we see in the night sky.

ICE CAPS Sheets of ice found at the north and south poles of Earth and Mars.

IMPACT CRATER A crater made by the impact (blow) of a meteorite.

INNER PLANETS The four planets relatively close together in the inner part of the solar system—Mercury, Venus, Earth, and Mars.

INTERPLANETARY Between the planets.

INTERSTELLAR Between the stars.

LAVA Molten rock that pours out of volcanoes.

LUNAR To do with the Moon.

MAGNETIC FIELD The region around a planet or a star in which its magnetism acts.

MANTLE A rocky layer beneath the crust of a rocky planet or moon.

METEOR A streak of light produced when a meteoroid burns up in Earth's atmosphere.

METEORITE A lump of rock from outer space that falls to the ground.

MINOR PLANETS Another name for the asteroids.

MOON   The common name for a satellite.

MORNING STAR   Usually the planet Venus seen in the eastern sky before sunrise. Mercury can also be a morning star.

NEBULA   A cloud of gas and dust in space.

ORBIT   The path in space one body follows when it circles around another, such as the Moon's orbit around Earth.

OUTER PLANETS   The planets in the outer part of the solar system—Jupiter, Saturn, Uranus, Neptune, and Pluto.

PHASES   The apparent changes in shape of Mercury, Venus, and the Moon in the sky. The changes come about because we see more or less of the surface of these bodies lit up by the Sun as time goes by.

PLANET   One of nine bodies that circle around the Sun; or more generally, a body that circles around a star.

PLATE TECTONICS   The science that deals with the movements of pieces, or plates, of Earth's crust.

PROBE   A spacecraft sent to explore other heavenly bodies, such as planets, moons, asteroids, and comets.

SATELLITE   A small body that orbits around a larger one; a moon. Also the usual name for an artificial satellite, an orbiting spacecraft.

SEA   A plain on the Moon, properly called mare.

SEASONS   Periods of the year marked by different temperatures and weather.

SHOOTING STAR   A popular name for a meteor.

SOLAR   To do with the Sun.

SOLAR SYSTEM   The Sun and the bodies that circle around it, including planets, comets, and asteroids.

STAR   A huge ball of very hot gas, which gives off energy as light, heat, and other radiation.

STELLAR   To do with the stars.

TERRESTRIAL   To do with Earth.

TERRESTRIAL PLANETS   The planets that are rocky like Earth—Mercury, Venus, and Mars.

TRANSIT   The crossing of the Sun's face, as viewed from Earth, by Mercury or Venus.

UNIVERSE   Space and everything that is in it—galaxies, stars, planets, moons, and energy.

VOLCANO   A hole, or crack in the ground, through which molten rock escapes.

Important Dates

150 Ptolemy of Alexandria sums up ancient astronomy, including the idea that Earth is the center of the universe with the Sun and planets circling round it

1543 Nicolaus Copernicus suggests a solar system

1610 Galileo spies the phases of Venus

1631 Astronomers observe first transit of Mercury

1639 Astronomers observe first transit of Venus

1704 Mars's polar ice caps discovered

1877 Asaph Hall discovers Mars's two moons Phobos and Deimos, Giovanni Schiaparelli reports seeing "canals" on Mars

1894 Percival Lowell builds the Lowell Observatory to study Mars

1916 Alfred Wegener in Germany introduces the idea of continental drift

1957 *Sputnik 1* becomes Earth's first artificial satellite, or moon

1962 *Mariner 2* becomes the first probe to investigate a planet—Venus

1965 The *Mariner 4* probe sends back the first close-up images of a planet—Mars

1967 The *Venera 4* probe parachutes into Venus's atmosphere

1974 The *Mariner 10* probe flies to Mercury, via Venus

1976 Two Viking probes land on Mars

1990 The Magellan probe maps Venus in detail

1996 NASA scientists suggest that a Martian meteorite contains microfossils

1997 Pathfinder probe and Sojourner rover land on Mars

2001 *Mars Odyssey* probe launched to orbit Mars

Further Reading

Large numbers of books on astronomy and space are available in school and public libraries. Librarians will be happy to help you find them. In addition, publishers display their books on the Internet, and you can key into their websites and search for astronomy books. Alternatively, you can look at the websites of on-line bookshops (such as Amazon.com) and search for books on astronomy and space. Here is just a selection of recently published books for further reading.

Backyard Astronomy by Robert Burnham, Time-Life 2001

Comet Science by Jacques Crovisier and Therese Encrenaz, Cambridge, 1999

Exploring the Night Sky with Binoculars by Patrick Moore, Cambridge, 2000

Field Guide to Stars and Planets by Jay Pasachoff, Houghton Mifflin, 1999

Get a Grip on Astronomy by Robin Kerrod, Time-Life, 1999

Introduction to Astronomy by Nick Shaffer, Random House, 1999

Night Sky by Gary Mechler, National Audubon Society, 1999

Observing the Moon by Peter Wlasuk, Springer, 1999

Target Earth by Duncan Steel, Time-Life, 2000

The Young Astronomer by Sheila Snowden, EDC Publications, 2000

Websites

Astronomy and space are popular topics on the Internet, and there are hundreds of interesting websites—details about the latest eclipse, mission to Mars and SETI (Search for Extraterrestrial Intelligence), and so forth.

A good place to start is by using a Search Engine, and search for space and astronomy. Search engines will display extensive listings of topics, which you can then select. For example, you gain access to a list of topics on the Search Engine Yahoo on astronomy with: **http://yahoo.com/Science/Astronomy**

The lists also include astronomy clubs. If there is one near you, you may well like to join it. Most clubs have interesting programs, with observing evenings, lectures, and visits to observatories.

NASA has many websites covering all aspects of space science, including exploration of the planets and the universe as a whole. The best place to start is at NASA's home page: **http://www.nasa.gov**

From there you can go to, for example, Space Science, which includes planetary exploration. Or you can go directly to: **http://spacescience.nasa.gov/missions**

Individual missions may also have their own website, such as the Mars Odyssey mission at: **http:/mars.jpl.nasa.gov/Odyssey**

The latest information and images from the Hubble Space Telescope can be reached at: **http:/www.stsci.edu/pubinfo** This site will also direct you to picture highlights since the launch of the Telescope in 1990.

European space science activities can be explored via the home page of the European Space Agency at: **http:/www.esa.int**

Index